His Love
Is Complete

A Compilation of
Love Poems, Short Stories, and other Libations from the Heart

His Love
Is Complete

A Compilation of
Love Poems, Short Stories, and other Libations of the Heart

V. Helena

Order this book online at www.trafford.com
or email orders@trafford.com

Most Trafford titles are also available at major online book retailers.

Trafford rev. 02/01/2012

 www.trafford.com

North America & international
toll-free: 1 888 232 4444 (USA & Canada)
phone: 250 383 6864 ♦ fax: 812 355 4082

For Rodney

Praise for *His Love is Freedom*

"V. Helena's writing reaches across mediums and offers spiritual nourishment for everyone, single and married alike. Whether you are fighting temptations or juggling occupations, you will find the strength to endure your circumstances. Indeed, you will hear from the Lord."

—Jamellah Ellis
author of That Faith, That Trust, That Love

"Honest and compelling."

—Kevin Wayne Johnson
author of the series Give God the Glory

"The exhortations of **His Love Is Freedom** were so insightful and compelling that we were inspired to use "The Glow of Love" and "Passionate Love" to help us express our appreciation to the women of our church. The reception and response were great, asking for more. **His Love Is Complete** is awesome in its message yet gentle in its stroking of heartstrings. *Sweet Aroma, Once,* and *I Remember When* are exceptional illustrations of the compatibility of love, passion and spirituality."

—Charles E. Pugh *Trustee,*
Vermont Avenue Baptist Church,
Washington, DC

Place me like a seal over your heart, like a seal on your arm;
for love is as strong as death, its jealousy unyielding as the grave.
Song of Songs 8:6

Love is patient,
  Love is kind.

    It does not envy,
      It does not boast,
        It is not proud.

It is not rude, it is not self-seeking, it is not easily angered, it keeps no record of wrongs.

        Love does not delight in evil,
but rejoices with the truth.

It always protects,
        Always trusts,
Always hopes,
        Always perseveres.

  Love never fails.

        1 Corinthians 13:4-8

Preface

What does it mean to love completely?

When you consider the scriptural definition of love in 1 Corinthians 13:4-8, the message is clear—love is an absolute. There are no loopholes, conditions, or limitations. God the Father (also referred to as Jehovah throughout this book) teaches us in this passage the true meaning of love. In this passage of scripture, He is teaching us what it means to love completely. How many of us are ready for a love like that?

Deciding to write a book on the journey one takes to find and keep love was certainly not an easy feat for me. I don't claim to be an expert on love and relationships (sometimes I'm as baffled as anyone else), however, as a relationship columnist, I've written about and have read a number of books on the subject, and I've had numerous discussions with couples and singles on their "love journey". The path to "true love" is certainly a maze full of booby traps, dead ends, endless trails, and ultimately the final reward on the other side IF one is able and willing to weather the seasons of love.

In my first book, ***His Love is Freedom: A Compilation of Spiritual Exhortations from the Heart,*** I focused on relaying the message that our vertical connection with Jehovah influences our relationship with others. In this book, I take the reader through various points in the Bible that clearly speaks of how you can manage through relationship challenges with the guidance of the word of God. I also provide insight on the topic based on interviews conducted with over 500 singles and couples in preparation of the publication. The Bible gives a number of references on how we should relate to each other if we are open to receiving these golden nuggets. ***His Love is Complete: A Compilation of Love Poems, Short Stories, and Other Libations from the Heart*** is specifically written for lovers and offers the notion of the journey of love as experienced through four distinct and vital seasons.

In books written by renowned relationship experts John Gray, Gary Chapman, Michelle McKinney Hammond, Kevin Leman, Barbara De Angelis, and Harville Hendrix they discuss the various phases of a relationship. I refer to these phases as seasons, and reference the Song of Songs as a backdrop to illustrate those seasons. I chose the Song of Songs for two reasons—1) because I'm intrigued by the story of King Solomon and his relationship with God, his people, and his women; and, 2) because I'm a helpless romantic and appreciate the love story told within the pages of this book.

In reading the story of King Solomon in 1 Kings 1 thru 11, we learn that he was the son of King David and had a wonderful relationship with God. His story chronicles that of a man who, in the beginning, steadfastly sought to please God, however, greed and idol worship disconnected him from his love relationship with God. In 1 Kings 3:6, we learn that King Solomon asked God for a discerning heart to govern the people of Israel. God was so pleased with this request that Solomon also received honor and riches the world over (1 Kings 3:6-15). With these gifts, God warned Solomon to be steadfast on the path of righteousness, avoiding the path of immorality and idolatry. Through the course of King Solomon's reign, he amassed great fortune and fame. Much of his fortune came through treaties with foreign countries, which usually included a marriage to the daughters of those principalities. It is said that he had many wives and concubines—1,000 to be exact! God's displeasure with Solomon rested in his disobedience to serve only one God. Many of his wives worshipped pagan gods, and his connection with them eventually turned his heart away from God. A very sad ending to such a promising beginning.

At first blush, you may believe the Song of Songs is the story of two lovers, and you're right! Many theologians and philosophers believe that it not only captures the spirit of Solomon's courtship and marriage to a Shulamite woman, it is also an illustration of God's love for his people. The book illustrates the joys and pains of Solomon's relationship with his beloved as they seek to find an unwavering spiritual love connection. The same is true in God's continued quest to win the love of his people. In this context, God is the Lover and we are his Beloved. Upon reading this love story and considering God's definition of love as noted in 1 Corinthian 13:4-8, I found the Song of Songs earnestly reflects the triumphs and challenges that are inherent in finding and sustaining a true love relationship. The entire book of Songs tells a wonderful story and I encourage you to meditate on these scriptures to reflect on your own journey to finding love.

Using the Song of Songs as the foundation for this book, the phases of love are symbolically portrayed within the four seasons of nature (Spring, Summer, Fall, and Winter). I think it is important to note that our relationships are constantly transitioning between seasons. Whether you are meeting someone for the first time, or have been married for 35 years, your relationship will continue its evolution through the seasons of love. It is through these transitions that love is tested and reaffirmed.

Spring is the first season of love and is full of the newness and excitement of the initial connection. We meet someone for the first time and we're excited about the possibilities. If your heart is open, you may even fall in love. If you are in a long-term relationship, this season may bring with it new experiences to share and store as memories. *Summer* sizzles as we engulf ourselves in the second season of love. It is full of passion and we are united in our love for one another. We spend quality time together, and are connected on the fundamentals of life. It is in this season that new couples firmly commit to each other. In the well-established relationship, this season allows the couple to continue moving to a higher degree of understanding within the relationship. I describe the passion contained within this season as a "celestial connection"—soul mates that are laboring in love. The third season, **Fall,** is one that many of us would rather avoid, but must go through in order to grow. It is disruptive, challenging and rooted in disappointment and heartbreak. The relationship will either die on the vine or champion those obstacles into a renewed commitment. **Winter** is a time of devotion and reflection. In this fourth and final season of love, we are steadfast in our connection and are a living testament to the staying power of a true love relationship.

It took four years to pull this body of work together. I very much appreciate those who shared their sincere thoughts and experiences with me. Some of you were settling into new relationships, while others of you have been celebrating love for over 40 years. Your personal stories were both enlightening and inspiring. What I appreciate most about this book is that it chronicles some of my own experiences, many of which I needed to go through in order to produce a heartfelt and sincere take on the seasons of love. My prayer is that you will glean from my experiences and of others shared in this book as you celebrate the universal language of love.

Finally, no matter what season you find yourself in, **never stop believing in love!**

Peace and love eternal,
V

"How great is the love the Father has lavished on us, that we should be called children of God! And that is what we are!" —1 John 3:1

Table of Exhortations

Winter: Devoted In Love

Pleasing is the fragrance of your perfumes; your name is
like perfume poured out. No wonder the maidens love you!
Song of Songs 1:3–Beloved

Your lips drop sweetness as the honeycomb, my bride; milk and
honey are under your tongue.
Song of Songs 4:11–Lover

Spring: Falling In Love

There is nothing sweeter than the fragrance of love brought in by the welcoming breeze of Spring. The warmth after the frost of Winter can conjure renewed clarity in an old relationship, or the exciting prospects of a new one. In Song of Songs 1:3 and 4:11 above, you can almost feel the genuine excitement and appreciation the Lover has for his Beloved. Everything about the beloved is enchanting—her lips, his smell, her taste, his name. Intoxicating!

Spring is a season of transition. It brings with it a sense of renewal and life. When two people meet and are attracted to one another, they dance to a rhythm that is uniquely theirs. It's a dance of promise and enticing possibilities. The same is true for couples who have weathered a tumultuous storm and have found themselves on the other side of that experience. Not only does it bring them closer in their connection, it further defines the relationship and adds depth to the dance.

This collection of work focuses on the beginning and renewed stages of love. Whether the blooms are sprouting from seedlings or are perennials making their yearly debut, the sweetness of a requited love can be exciting as much as it is fulfilling.

How beautiful you are, my darling!
Oh, how beautiful!
Your eyes behind your veil are doves.
Song of Songs 4:1

Flowers appear on the earth;
the season of singing has come,
the cooing of doves is heard in our land.
Song of Songs 1:12

You are a garden locked up, my sister,
my bride;
You are a spring enclosed, a sealed fountain.
Song of Songs 4:12

The Glow Of Love

Like a red rose glistening from the morning dew,
love blossomed with the warmth of the spring sunshine . . .
caressing itself in the shelter of its womb . . .
finding nirvana in the sweet, softness of your heated whispers.

How can I tell you how much "love" has meant to me?
. . . to show you how saying "yes" has set me free?
Liberated by the power of a stare . . .
the intensity of a touch . . .
the passion of liquid kisses . . .

My heated vessel encloses a life source
that can only exist in your presence.

My world is now colored with songs of laughter and solitude.
Alas, I am a work of art!
. . . laboring in your love.

A Prayer For You

A young woman once prayed,
"Father, when the time is right
direct me to he who is perfectly and exquisitely made for me.
Dipped in honey
flavored by your goodness,
Good-natured, spirit-led, smart and funny,
Steadfastly walking in your fullness."

"Until then, my service is your pleasure. Only help me to see he who
is divinely made for me."

A young man once prayed,
"Almighty Father, make me a warrior for thee,
Cloak me in your protection,
Shield me from negative direction.
Help me discern that which is not of you.
Focus me to be all that you want from me."

"And when the time is right,
steer me to she
who is divinely and exquisitely made for me."

On a very special day
At the appointed time,
When neither were looking or hoping,
The two did meet.
He recognized her and their union was so sweet.

Just For Me

I dreamed it, I prayed on it, and I believed in it.
At first dawn, I only caught a glimpse of what could be.
But by sunrise, it was blaringly clear . . .

A mate just for me . . .
              just for me.

New life . . . new hope . . . new beginnings . . .
Spring is symbolic of the newness of our life and journey together.

May God continue to bless, guide, and nurture our union . . .
my husband, my wife . . .
        my friend, my life.

After You . . .

Driving through the busy downtown streets of Washington D.C. like a New York cabbie in rush hour was not going to get me to the office any faster. A ticket maybe, an accident involving a pedestrian likely, but definitely not at my desk in 10 minutes. I should've caught the bus, but I woke up too late for that. Geez! I set the alarm, even woke up for my usual 5am bio break, but here I am racing through the streets praying Father Time will give me a break. On top of that, I'm going to have to pay an exorbitant downtown D.C. parking fee. I can hear Momma in my head telling me in her island soaked voice, *get your rumpas 'n the bed at a decent 'our and there won't be no trouble.* Easy for her to say! She never had to work ungodly hours or suffered from insomnia.

Driving into the parking garage, I moaned a sigh of relief when I saw no sign of the boss man's car in its reserved parking spot.

"Great!" I thought as I grabbed my briefcase and sprinted over to the elevator bank before my luck changed. Eric, our new CEO, is usually in the office at least two hours by the time I roll out of bed. He expects everyone to follow suit, which is hard when you're working 12 hour days with a regularity. Pressing the button for the second floor, I heard Momma chiding, "*Let 'em tink you're the last one out. Tat's gonna get ya far up da food chain.* How long would I have to keep up that schedule before it pays off?

"Good Morning, Lena," the "too sexy for my shoes" summer intern said before throwing up her index finger and tending to the phone system, which lit up like a Christmas tree all the sudden.

"Hey, Bridget. Is Eric here?" I inquired after she came up for air.

Completely oblivious to any confidences that may have been compromised in divulging such information, Bridget proceeded to give me a five minute run down on the drama that transpired between Eric and his wife the night before. Eric called it an "unforeseen circumstance". We called it a shame. Bridget went back to answering the phones as I headed to my office contemplating how I could get away with using Eric's parking spot for the remainder of the week.

Dropping my briefcase on the desk and checking my schedule, I suddenly had the cursed urge for a café libation from the new coffee shop across the street. I could almost smell those heavenly beans from my second floor window. After 20 minutes of checking email and trying to shake the thought from my head, I got mad when I realized I could have gone and been back in that time! I grabbed my purse and headed for the door while Momma's chastisement followed closely on my heels. *Just becuz the boss man is out don't mean you gotta be cute.*

As I was about to grab hold of the door handle to mocha latte paradise, it opened from the inside and right smack front and center was the most gorgeous man I'd ever laid eyes on. A chocolate drop from heaven! An athletic build on this 6'0 frame, the angel wore a fitted navy Armani suit accented with a reddish-gold *la corbata*. The chisel in his chin, the perfect alignment of his pearly whites, and the slight squint of his eyes seeking protection from the sunlight left me speechless, and that was a good thing. I took him in like an inviting bowl of cherries, and the last thing I needed to do was talk with my mouth full.

"After you," the sun demigod finally uttered with an expression that made my heart do that fluttery thing, which was cut short when I heard that annoying voice from Momma rocking in my head. *Keep it movin', young lady. Don't eat all 'our cookies in one sitting!*

"Thanks." I said catching a waft of Davidoff's Cool Water dancing from his skin. I quickly made note of his left-hand before unlocking my trance. I've embarrassed myself in the past by not paying attention to the "left-2ⁿᵈ-digit" and now was no time for a let down. Momma didn't raise no fool.

Mr. "Fine-As-Hell" proceeded to step aside as I sashayed into the caffeine lair of addiction. I wanted so badly to turn around for one last peek at this incredible man, but doing that would certainly have Momma's voice in my head for a good part of the day. I took in the sights and sounds and briefly considered my waistline, which was unforgiving when it came to the new habit. I smiled graciously and waited my turn at the trough.

"Tall, Black Mocha," I bellowed, giggling at my private joke. So fitting that I would like my drink the way I prefer my men. A string of relationships with all flavors and sizes always brought me back to that truth. I've decidedly and happily rested in my fate.

"$4.95," bellowed the caramel frap taking my order. Just as I was opening my wallet, Cool Water splashed all over me and just like Christmas in July, a navy blue arm reached from behind and produced a twenty. So close was he that I was sure I had been dipped in chocolate!

I paused and waited for Momma's voice. Nothing. She decided to let her daughter go this one alone. So, I took a quick moment to gather myself before turning around slowly and extending my hand.

"Thank you very much . . . Lena."

"Victor," he said as he stuffed his change into his wallet. Again, I checked the ring finger just to be sure I wasn't tripping.

"Do you have a minute?" he said flashing a disarming, megawatt grin while tilting his head and stroking his goatee. Dang, he looked good enough to swallow whole!

"I might have two," I said grabbing my cup and trying to maintain composure for fear Momma may make another appearance.

"After you," Victor said with a gesture towards an empty table. His eyes took me in full and hard leaving no room for guessing what might've been going on in that perfectly round, bald dome. I giggled at Momma's silence surely put off by his blatant approval of my assets.

As we sipped on our gourmet delights, exchanged pleasantries and numbers, and took in every syllable and movement, I thanked God for waking up late and "unforeseen circumstances". I thanked Him for latte addictions and chocolate drop dreams. I thanked Him for aligning moments to spare with good conversation. I thanked Him for a Momma's voice from beyond that still speaks in the still of life. I thanked Him for a Momma that taught me His ways, which echoes in me always.

*You have stolen my heart, my sister, my bride; you have stolen my heart with
one glance of your eyes, with one jewel of your necklace.
Song of Songs 4:9–Lover*

*I belong to my lover, and his desire is for me.
Song of Songs 7:10–Beloved*

Summer: United In Love

After enjoying the warmth and admiring the blooms of Spring, it's time to turn up the heat with the hot sizzling days of Summer. By the time a couple reaches this season of love, they have established a commitment to one another and are coming into a deeper understanding of themselves in the relationship.

What I appreciate most about the passages noted above is the obvious affection shared between the Lover and Beloved. The lover makes clear his intentions, and the beloved responds in acknowledgement and acceptance. Think of your own relationship and the blissful assurance in knowing you and your intended are of the same mind and of one accord.

This collection of work translates the language of a united and kindled love—one of promise, curiosity, and abandon. When based in sincerity and earnest, the love shared between two people can be an elixir for the soul. It ignites the fire within, serving as confirmation to Jehovah's promise in providing for our heart's desire.

I am my lover's and my lover is mine;
he browses among the lilies.
Song of Songs 6:3

How handsome you are, my darling!
Oh, how charming!
And our bed is verdant.
Song of Songs 1:16

Take me away with you— let us hurry!
Let the king bring me into his chamber.
Song of Songs 1:4

My lover is to me a sachet of myrrh resting between my breasts.
My lover is to me a cluster of henna blossoms
from the vineyards of En Gedi.
Song of Songs 1:13-14

Once . . .
(for Rodney)

A heated whisper.
Cascaded down and around
my aroused neck.
Penetrated my soul.
Plowed deep into my heart.
Held my name hostage . . .
Once . . .

A soft, liquefied kiss.
Heated with desire.
Ignited by fire.
Claiming the Ying to my Yang.
The Alpha and Omega sang . . . to me . . .
Once . . .

An embrace.
Purposeful and meaningful.
Truthful and undeniable.
Held me longingly . . . lovingly . . . perpetually . . .
Once . . .

Once . . .
I was alone.
Walking proudly and confidently . . .
Until you came along.
Stopped me in my tracks.
Trained me how to walk in step with you.
Showed me what a true whisper, kiss, and embrace could do.
When gifted by one so pure in heart and virtue.
Many are the treasures I have found in you.

Sweet Aroma

Oh, how sweet is the aroma of your smile!
Like the silky and delicate touch of a rose petal,
Your laughter fills me with titillating elation—
Only surpassed by the warmth of your touch . . . upon my bosom.

Oh, how sweet is the aroma of your kiss!
Your intoxicating tête-à-tête explores the uncharted waters of my
intellect,
Causing streams of calming waters where there was once rapids!

Created so divinely by He who promised to give my hearts desire,
Let me not be intoxicated with my own thoughts . . .
But let me fuel the embers of my heart with the knowledge that this
time is ordained.
Our love will sustain.

The absence of your presence is never felt
because the sweetness of your aroma lingers . . .
Always.

A Delight

As I close my honey brown windows and allow the sun to gently
caress my face
Each beautiful ray dances whimsically around me . . . soothing all the
same
Kneeding, prodding, contemplating the destiny of this cocooned
pillar
Transitioning for first flight . . .
What a delight . . . a delight.

I caress the newness of your touch
One that is familiar, but new all the same
New hope, new desires, new places to teleport . . .
Reaching new heights . . .
What a delight . . . a delight.

I relax in the rhythm of your dance
Mind blowing moves, but gentle all the same
A connection so right, no one can tell me it's wrong,
Gonna hold on to this good thing with all my might . . .
Gonna do it until we get it right . . .
Not gonna worry if it takes all night . . .
What a delight . . . a delight!

Perfectly & Divinely Yoked

Two souls . . .
One path . . .
The appointed time.

A special prayer went forth,
A heart's desire conceived.
Vessels bound in faith, hope, and love,
were reciprocally received.

Gingerly ordered,
My steps lead me to you.
Cloaked with His promise . . .
Orchestrated by His kindness . . .
Strengthened by His greatness.
On this day,
I pledge my forever with you.

Like a quiet storm,
Our love will beautifully illuminate through the darkest of hours.
And with the morning sunshine, bring forth dandelions and daffodils
with splendor and power.

Purposefully . . .
Divinely . . .
Perfectly Yoked.
Guarded in His grace . . .
Sanctioned by His love . . .
Blessed by our faith . . .
Truly a gift from above.

Imperfect, BUT Perfect for Each Other

Shaking his head in disgust, Cory Foster took the coffee mug from his wife's extended hand.

"Can you believe this guy? The buffoonery begins!"

"You're looking at the next governor of the great state of Maryland," Venus chided as her husband grunted in agreement. They looked on as footage from an interview with Maryland State Governor hopeful, Jim Robbins, played out on their wide screen TV.

"As much as I hate to admit it, I guess you're right. I don't agree with everything he stands for, but he's definitely a better candidate than Riley," Cory said as he took a sip of his coffee.

"And the constituency apparently loves him. He's a good margin over Riley in the polls," Venus chimed as she sashayed into the dressing room in a fourth attempt at finding an outfit suitable for the afternoon tea she was scheduled to attend. Cory proceeded to put on his tie as he assessed his wife's comment.

"I'm not sure who their polling, but I do know the people of Maryland are a lot smarter than the media reports. The bigger question is where does his running mate stand on the issues. He's as quiet as a church mouse."

Venus smiled as she watched her husband's eyebrows furrow in contemplation.

"Well, Congressman Foster. Perhaps you can get him to comment on the issues at next week's Chamber of Commerce dinner. No mics . . . no cameras. Just the two of you enjoying dinner in mixed company. Perhaps he'll be a little more forthcoming."

Cory grinned as he watched Venus emerge from the closet with the Jacques Charles suit he bought her a few weeks ago. Gazing at her fondly, he could feel his nature rise as he took in the silhouette of her firm body loosely draped in a Kimono robe that subtly exposed a red, lace panty and bra set. Cory shook his head and silently thanked God for coming through on his promise to provide his heart's desire. Not only did Venus take very good care of herself physically, her razor sharp insight made her as attractive today as it did 17 years ago when they met. Cory couldn't get over how blessed he was.

"Has Junior left for school?" he said watching intently as Venus slid on her lace thigh-high stockings.

"He left while you were in the shower. Mumbled something about getting in early to finish his Science project."

The mention of their son conjured a proud smile on Cory's face. His political ambitions came with great sacrifice, yet he couldn't be more proud of his son and his accomplishments. A straight A-student and athlete, Cory Junior had grown to be everything his father had hoped. College bound within a few months, it was sometimes hard for Cory to believe how quickly time had slipped away and yet he couldn't help but feel a tinge of guilt in not being present when he thought it counted. The Saturday afternoon basketball games, the back-to-school nights, the swim tournaments—all counted as a loss due to campaign and office obligations. As the memories fleetingly came to mind, he smiled as he watched the woman who kept it all together struggle with her skirt zipper.

"You need a hand with that," he said as he slowly walked behind her and unzipped the skirt.

"I was trying to zip it up, Love," Venus said shooing his hands away.

"I should be able to take the weekend off . . . maybe we can drive up to Cape May," Cory said wrapping his arms around her waist and nibbling on her ear.

"Oh . . . really," Venus giggled as she playfully struggled to release his grip, causing her backside to gently brush against his growing erection.

"Hmmm . . . but what about work, Love?" Venus said with a sly smile.

"I'm thinking I can move a couple of things out to next week to allow for a work free weekend as long as I can carry my blackberry," he said while removing her bra with the precision of a magician.

"Blackberry is still my friend. I haven't kicked her out yet." Venus turned around and wrapped her arms around her husband's neck as he gently lifted her up onto the vanity table.

Cory checked his watch and grinned. "I'm not really due in the office for another hour and a half. That should be just enough time to start the weekend off right."

"That sounds like a plan, baby," Venus whispered softly as her husband's hands methodically explored the softness of her body until she moaned with pleasure. She felt her husband's beard brush gently down her neck as he softly planted heated kisses on her shoulder. She took in the scent of his designer aftershave and felt the energy of his passion embrace every fiber of her being. Surrendering, she closed her eyes as the power of his love washed over her.

From the vanity table, to the chaise, to finally their marital bed, they moved to the familiar rhythm of their love. A love rooted in a passion for one another spawned from the pain and joy of their life together. Two years as college soul mates and fifteen years of marriage presented many obstacles and rewards. Through the death of parents, the birth of their son, the pain of an extramarital affair, and the triumph in meeting professional pursuits they have worked through each challenge and accomplishment as partners—imperfect, but perfect for each other. A knowing that the other is committed to the journey and all that comes with it. Spirits intertwined and experiencing the true meaning of a requited love.

Fall: Divided In Love

Although we all hate to go through it, there comes a time in every relationship when love will be challenged and tested. In the end, the couple will either grow having gone through the trial, or they will find the foundation of their love is not strong enough to withstand the tumultuous storm that has steered in their path.

The Fall season signals the end of the sweet passion of Summer, and is the prelude to the restorative attributes of Winter. It is in this stage that a couple experiences the "great divide". Challenges related to money, raising children, relating to in-laws and other family situations, friendships outside of the relationship, career and academic goals, and communicating with each other are among the topics that reveal fundamental differences and philosophies. Fall is a transitional season that threatens to change the course of the earlier season while holding the keys to the promise of the succeeding season. Fall provides an opportunity for change, growth, and hope. It is a time for love to hang on with purpose and earnest.

In the Song of Songs 3:1-2, Beloved laments with a heavy heart laden with disappointment in the current state of the relationship. The disappointment is difficult to conceive given the fire that roared with promise not to long ago. How many of us have been in that place? If you made it through, certainly you can understand how difficult (but necessary) that transition was in getting to a higher level of love and acceptance.

The body of work in this section seeks to invoke the spirit of patience, faith, encouragement and mercy in preparing for the transitional days of a love experiencing "the Fall".

Tell me, you whom I love, where you graze your flock
and where you graze your sheep at midday.
Song of Songs 1:7

Catch for us the foxes, the little foxes that ruin the vineyards,
our vineyards that are in bloom.
Song of Songs 2:15

Daughters of Jerusalem, I charge you by the gazelles and by the does
of the field: Do not arouse or awaken love until it so desires.
Song of Songs 3:5

I Remember When

At what point does the heart yield?
Actually stops fighting and puts down the shield?
Terse words with high meaning.
Silent table talk now replaces exuberant indulgence.

"No!" The heart counsels. "We need to control this thang!"
"Need to let God enter in
to smooth away the pain."
"I want . . . No . . . I *need* love to freely
play with me."

And with no regrets,
Love learned its lesson for the day
With promises only beholden to thee who stays.
Slowly the heart turned back, laughed, and confidently chimed,
". . . I remember when."

Why Do I Stay?

Because you're truly not like the rest . . .
Because you take me beyond my limits to my greatest potential . . .
Because you elevate my senses when I'm at my lowest of times . . .
Because you trust me beyond what you thought was ever possible . . .
Because I can grow without judgment in your eyes . . .
Because I'm filled with the knowledge that you have my back, front,
side, top . . .
Because you're confident enough to appreciate that I'm not going to
put up or shut up about whatever you're dishing out . . .
Because you can lean on me and know I won't let you fall.

On any given day, any of these would suffice
But when it comes right down to why you're in my life . . .

I stay . . . because being without you is not an option to my heart.

Candles, Coltrane, and You

Silky waters, dancing lights, and sips of cooling springs
Dependable delights that soothe and entice . . . me
Pleasurable dreams of thoughts that supply . . . me
With mind thirsty decadence
and thoughtful recompense.

Delicious, lofty, tunes fill the room
With hues of antique white and gray
That causes shadows to move and sway
To the heart of yesterday
Beating as fast as the wind will carry . . . us.

Oh, how blessed I am to share this moment in space
With a mate who has also been touched by grace
And understands the significance of His glory
Who knows and also believes in His story

One who will take my hand sincerely and purposefully with
love . . . honor . . . forgiveness . . . understanding
healing . . . support . . . hope, notwithstanding
all He has promised and will certainly deliver.

Oh, how I anticipate the day,
When the musician will play,
To an empty crowd waiting to be filled with a gift
that only the Father can provide
Notes as fluid as the ocean will carry . . . me
To my final destiny.

Embracing the Process

I was OK with seeing him today.
The conversation was not stressed.
The emotions were checked, but at best, I was a wreck.
Hard to release him from my system.
Hard to let go of what once promised to be right,
although with further insight and prayerful consideration,
a continued relationship was not part of the Father's equation.

Torn but not broken,
I must go through the process of seeking Him more,
and wanting him less.

Destiny

You don't ask for much . . .
Only the basics in life.
Food, water, shelter, and a rub on the tummy when life's challenges
emerge now and then,
Such a good companion . . . such a great friend.

I tell you my stories and you listen intently with eyes wide and
curious.
Wondrous mysteries to behold,
Such history in that soul.

You wait patiently and thoughtfully,
Focused and knowingly.
I know it, too!
The fallout is inevitable . . . undeniable.

Tracing back my steps to discover what, why, and how is pointless.
Alas, the season of change.
I'm following your lead into what's destined to be.

Right Before Take Off

Right before take-off, the flight attendants go through safety and emergency procedures with the passengers. On the off chance that I'm paying attention, I always found it disconcerting that they would instruct you to put on your oxygen mask before helping someone else with theirs. My natural instinct made me feel uncomfortable about that because I am usually putting others before myself. I now realize the importance of securing my own mask first. Before I can help someone else, I have to make sure I'm ok . . . I have to make sure I can breathe. I'm taking this "break" to breathe.

I'm not sure how to explain it, but I knew I was connected to you the moment I saw you . . . or perhaps it happened during our phone calls or emails. I don't know exactly when anymore . . . everything is cloudy. I DO know that when I saw you standing there waiting outside the entrance of what would later be our favorite restaurant, I recognized your spirit. I saw you . . . and I knew I had finally found my way home. After all the hiccups and false starts, it happened. After all the bad connections and painful disconnections, I knew that I had finally found what I needed in you.

Through the course of our relationship, we have shared our pain and found healing through each other, but for some reason today . . . I'm struggling to breathe. This latest challenge has stretched me beyond my capacity to forgive! I have never been so wronged in my life, so how can I even conceive overcoming this level of pain?

Has anyone seen my love? Certainly, you are not him. He would never have treated me this way. I have asked myself several times WHY ARE YOU DIFFERENT? Why can't I just walk away? Why does the thought of walking away conjure such sorrow, yet staying causes such pain? I know in my heart that I will move beyond this latest transgression to find love in you again. I don't want to accept it right now, but I know it will be.

I am wittingly enslaved. I don't know where this road will lead, but the fact remains. I can't imagine a life without you . . . I'm putting on my oxygen mask.

Can He Fix This?

"Hello."

"I'm leaving him."

"What?"

"It's after 11:00 and I haven't heard from him since this morning."

Wendy sat up in her bed and reached for the lamp. It was day three of Angie's latest challenge with Kevin and she knew this was not going to be a quick and easy conversation. Angie was her best friend and sorority sister, and was there when Angie met her husband, Kevin, 12 years ago. She stood as maid-of-honor when they married five years later and is the god-mother of their 7-year old daughter, Kia. Hearing about Kevin's behavior within the last two days made Wendy feel like hitting him upside the head with a bag of nickels herself, but she decided to reserve that offer as a possible solution for another day.

"Have you tried calling him? Maybe something happened."

"I'm pretty sure nothing has happened. He wouldn't answer the phone if I called anyway. All the sudden he doesn't answer the phone when he's out, which really pisses me off!" Angie said angrily.

"This just doesn't sound like Kevin. What's gotten in to him?" Wendy said rubbing her eyes.

"I'll tell you what's gotten into him. He has lost his damn mind! I tell you, Wendy, I'm done. This is it! I can't go on living like this. I mean, what the hell is he thinking? I'm just supposed to sit here and take this crap?"

"Did you two have another fight?"

"Yes. For the exact reason we argued about the other day. He claims to be working late hours, but this is ridiculous," Angie screamed into the phone. "Yesterday he smelled like cigarettes so he couldn't use that excuse on me. When I called him on it, he said he stopped at a bar near the office before coming home. By the time he got home, it was almost midnight.

I mean, who does that at his age? He has a child and responsibilities. He should have brought his selfish behind home!"

As Angie continued her tirade, Wendy reflected on their years of friendship. She loved Angie and Kevin as if they were kin. She really didn't want to get caught in the middle of their quarrel, but knew it was inevitable. Of course, Angie shared other issues she and Kevin have had through the years, but this recent impasse just didn't make sense to Wendy. She knew Kevin would never cheat on Angie and hoped her girlfriend wasn't even thinking along those lines. Wendy weighed the possibility of a drinking problem, but held off on that thought until she was certain of the pattern. She knew this latest challenge between them would pass, as did the others. Wendy said a silent prayer asking God to use her in this situation.

"Wen, I'm sorry to bother you with all this, and I really appreciate you being here for me," Angie said in a more controlled tone as she slowly started to calm down after complaining about Kevin non-stop for what seemed like 10 minutes.

"I'm fine and I'm here for you, Angie. You mentioned yesterday that he's been working on the new municipal center project. That's a big effort! It has to be pretty stressful for him. Maybe he's stopping at the bar to unwind," Wendy said as she slipped on her bedroom slippers and robe.

"That's why I'm here! To help him deal with those stressors. We have always been that for each other. What's so different now? You think I don't know stress? Try getting a publication out every month that holds a readership of 8.5 million."

"This isn't a competition, Ang. We're talking about your husband and the support he may need from you right now." Wendy was trying not to be too firm with Angie, but at the same time she knew it was her job to give her sister-friend a kick in the pants when she started talking crazy. Turning on the light in the kitchen, she put a kettle on the fire and took in a deep breath. She had a feeling it was going to be a long night.

"Well, all I'm saying is he's been leaving for work at 4:30 in the morning and getting home later and later for the last few weeks. I know he has a lot on his plate, but he also has a daughter that would like to see her father from time to time, and a wife that needs to connect with him emotionally and physically. Three days ago, he started coming in after 10. Every night since, he's been coming in later and later. Wendy, it's damn near midnight! I mentioned something to him about it yesterday and now he's just doing it out of spite. And when he does finally get home, he doesn't say a word to me. He just takes a shower, gets in the bed, and turns his back on me. Then, after about five minutes, he's snoring. We have no connection between us right now at all . . . and I mean none. He doesn't seem to get that his family is a lot more important than making partner or some new project he's working on."

Wendy listened intently as Angie continued to point out other things that Kevin was doing that irritated and frustrated her. It began to sound as though Kevin couldn't do anything right in Angie's eyes, and knowing her girl, Wendy knew Angie was pretty vocal about that. She also knew Kevin had a low tolerance level for that kind of talk. She thought about how she could gently offer suggestions, then smiled suddenly when God delivered.

"I can only imagine how difficult this must be for you, Angie, and I want you to know I'm here for you. From what you've told me thus far, I believe Kevin is going through a tough time right now, and probably needs your support more than ever. Maybe he has temporarily lost sight of your role as his partner, friend, and confidant. Right now, it sounds as though he may be feeling more like an adversary if he's coming home to a potential fight. Do the two of you still pray together?"

Wendy could feel how disarming her question was for Angie. She knew the power of prayer and wondered why couples seldom share this practice with each other.

"We used to, but honestly we haven't prayed together in years," Angie said before blowing her nose.

"Ask God to fix your marriage, Angie. Put it in His hands . . . He can fix this."

"I can't even see him long enough to hold a conversation. How am I going to get him to pray with me?" Angie asked sincerely.

"Then start by praying for your husband and your marriage."

"I just don't know, Wendy."

"You could either start by praying for him or when he comes home tonight, takes his shower, and jumps in the bed, tap him on the shoulder and offer to pray before you go to sleep."

Wendy waited patiently as Angie silently considered her suggestion. She knew Angie was supportive of Kevin's career and dreams of opening his own firm. She shared in their joy as they both accomplished varying levels of success. Angie as a successful publisher of *Christian Living*, a Christian magazine voted #1 in circulation among other magazines of that genre, and Kevin as a sought-after architect on the verge of building a clientele that would finally establish him among the top in the country. Wendy knew with the trappings of success come great responsibility, which was even more a reason to gird up strength in the Lord. She realized that although her friends knew the Lord, everyone could stand to hear a reminder of His love and in his ability to move mountains. This latest challenge was their mountain. She only hoped they would view it as such and turn to Him for guidance.

"I hear what you're saying, Wen, but I feel in my heart of hearts that he is doing this just to get back at me. It's that stupid tit-for-tat thing that our relationship has been reduced too. Since when was it ever OK to not call when working later than usual? He just ticks me off so easily these days. He just doesn't get it."

Angie went on to tell Wendy how unfeeling Kevin appeared to be whenever she tried to talk to him, and how he didn't seem to care that he was spending less and less time with Kia. She also spoke of their upcoming family holiday gatherings and that he has flatly informed her that he would not be participating. Suddenly, Wendy began to realize this was a little more serious than she thought.

"Listen to me, Angie. Do not let the enemy drive a wedge between you and your husband," Wendy said firmly. "You know I know what I'm talking about. This isn't your friend the psychologist talking, this is a woman who knows the pain of a broken marriage."

Wendy gave her tears permission to fall as she thought of the demise of her own marriage five years ago. Although she reconciled the mistakes made with her husband, she still grieved the loss of his companionship. Reflecting now, she knew her marriage was "fixable", but she didn't have the tools she possessed now to put faith in God to strengthen her through those trials. She was determined to help her friend through this difficult time. If she didn't know anything else, she knew Angie loved her husband. She may not appreciate what he is doing, but she loved him and that was enough to turn the situation around.

"Talk to Kevin . . . not with the anger, but with the love you two have grown to have for each other. Find your way back to one another," Wendy said gently.

"Wen, you know I love Kevin with everything I got, but . . ."

"There are no conditions with love, Angie," Wendy interrupted. "There is no, *but*."

"I wish it was that simple," Angie said almost inaudibly.

"I know things feel really bad right now, and it may seem like leaving is the answer to everything, but believe me when I tell you it's not. Running away never solves the problem. Stay on course, sis. This time will pass, and when it does, the two of you will be stronger for it because you would have weathered this storm together."

"I really hope you're right about that," Angie said.

"I know I'm right. Will you promise me you'll pray on it and invite Kevin to pray with you?"

"I can do that."

"One more thing."

"What's that, sis?"

"Can we pray together right now?"

"I think I need that more than ever," Angie said with a sigh.

"Father, help us through this seemingly difficult time. Help us see beyond this situation in recognition of what it truly is . . . a challenge that we can overcome with your guidance. We believe you are with us as we face this immediate challenge. The devil is a liar and is forever trying to find a foothold in your plan. His attacks are endless and persistent. But heavenly Father, we acknowledge that he has no place here because we don't belong to him. Our debt was paid through the blood of Jesus. We pray that our actions and words will always be in edification of Your Word and Will. Thank you, Father, for the many blessings through experiences you have given us. We have come a long way and take solace in knowing that you have been with us every step of the journey. Please remind us of your continued walk with us when we feel otherwise. Please remind us that your love for us can get us through anything. Please help us to put aside our own selfish agendas to focus on the "we" and not the "me". Teach us, Father, to forgive as we have been forgiven in your sight. Bring my brother and sister to a place of understanding and remind them that they can look to you for healing in this circumstance. In Jesus our Savior and Redeemer, we pray this prayer of strength in the full knowledge that you are with us and will deliver us from this challenge. Amen."

"Amen. Honey, I thought you were going to pray, not preach."

"Did you receive it?"

"How could I not?"

"Then His message to you through me was not in vain."

"Thanks, sweetie. Again, I'm sorry I woke you. You're always there for me and I thank God for you."

"God is good!" Wendy put down her mug and raised her hands up in worship.

"I think I hear Kevin pulling up. I'll call you in the morning. Get some sleep, Sis. Thanks and I love you."

"I love you, too, sweetie. Goodnight."

Many waters cannot quench love; rivers cannot wash it away.
—Song of Songs 8:7—Beloved

Winter: Devoted In Love

Finally, Winter. The season of renewal. The passage above refers to the enduring power of love. Through all the challenges, love never gives up . . . it always prevails. "Waters cannot quench [nor] rivers wash it away". It endures forever.

As we face challenges in our Christian walk, it is good to have a partner who has vowed to walk this road with us. Receiving an encouraging word or a hand of support from your life partner can make all the difference in the world. It strengthens our bond and devotion to each other. Folding that under the guidance and protection of the Father creates an unmovable, unshakeable bond that is destined to endure the winds and storms of time.

Like any relationship, there will be times when love will not cooperate. Like an unruly child, it will fight and wreak havoc. Given all the strife it can bring, it's good to know that if we stay focused on Jehovah's love and promises for our life, He will sustain us in any challenge, including those that we face in our love relationships.

The following is a collection of affirmation and encouragement for love in the season of renewal and commitment. It's time to celebrate because you've made it through the storms of life and are reaping the benefits of a stronger and more fulfilling love!

My lover spoke and said to me,
'Arise, my darling,
My beautiful one, and come with me.
Song of Songs 2:10

Let us go early to the vineyards
To see if the vines have budded,
If their blossoms have opened,
And if the pomegranates are in bloom—
There I will give you my love.
Song of Songs 7:12

If one were to give all the wealth of his house for love,
It would be utterly scorned.
Song of Songs 8:7

I Told You!

There it goes again!
Did you hear that?
Did you hear that roaring thunder clap?!
Such a horrific noise the heart makes.

And just like before, it causes a quake
In my knees, in my heart, in the corner creases of my mind
A hurtful penetrating ache.

What a brilliant sound it is!
Causes me to stand at attention.
Not to mention
The building cry within threatening to release once again.
The resounding yes of requited love and an absolve to recompense.

I TOLD YOU!
The heart finally bellows
Before it settles in quiet satisfaction.

A false start before reality set in and inevitably took action once again.
No need to fetter
Enjoy the thunderclap in the wind.
The Father is in the midst holding it together
And until then . . .

I TOLD YOU!

I'm Reminded

You remind me of a lukewarm breeze scented by the honeysuckle dew
of Spring;
A young girl's dream of "FAME" and wanting to live forever;
Long walks in pleasant thoughts and chamomile dreams promising a
goodnights rest.

You remind me of Saturday mornings
Warm mocha milk on frosty days
And cares that are cast away temporarily, but assuredly.

Oh, what I wouldn't do to get back
to when you reminded me of the fact
that I am whole because of you not an extension of another.
I'm reminded . . . yet . . .

Passionate Love

Ours is a passionate love.
Lined with lavender and jasmine oils,
scented candles,
walks on pink sands,
talks under moonlit skies,
dreams of forever times,
and hopes of peaceful and loving hearts.

Ours is a passionate love.
Etched with silent stares,
crumpled tissue,
raised eyebrows and voices,
hard choices and swallowed thoughts and pride,
bouts of alone time and struggles inside.
Rainy days
cast away
as nonchalantly as they came.

Ours is a passionate love,
that sees beyond the sunshine and rain,
rejuvenates,
and make whole again
in the oneness and fulfillment that God can only bring,
when two come together and with a joyful noise sing.
His praises . . . because
His passionate love endures forever.

I Am Still

Softly your aura fills me. I am captive . . . I am still.

Your peacefulness calms my active spirit . . . what needs to follow is the will.

I am captive . . . I am still.

That's *How We Roll!*

Lord, help me if that woman says, Amen, one more time. She's been talking me and Michael's ear off since we got here. I don't know why church folks feel it necessary to put on airs around the leadership and demonstrate how "holy" they are when we are within earshot. Amen this, and Amen that. I'm willing to bet "Amen" doesn't escape her lips any other time but supper time under usual circumstances.

I so dread being dragged to the AME Leadership Conference every year. And I'm so sick of these nosy women who want to know what's going on in our personal life, so that the moment they suspect some drama, they try to move in for the kill. I have had to deal with that the better part of 25 years since Michael started his ministry.

The old days were so much simpler. We had a small church of about 20 people, not the 55,000 we tend to now. My older son, Mickey, was just a teenager back then, and his younger brother, Ezra, couldn't have been more than five. Now Ezra is about to do his trial sermon in a few weeks as Michael grooms him to become the next pastor of Jehovah AME. Mickey didn't want to follow in his Daddy's footsteps, but he sure is making out well for himself as a big time executive for IBM. We are all so proud of him. We're proud of both of our boys and their success in life. Ezra will more than likely marry Joanne, although I would have preferred Rose Mary if he had asked me, but he didn't. I guess anybody is better than Mickey's wife, Claudette, but there isn't much I can do about that either.

Whooooo! This woman can talk. Mouth goin' a mile a minute! I think she said her name is Brenda or Clenda . . . I don't know. I'll just nod and smile like a usually do. I'd fail the test with a big zero if I have to recap what's she's saying. Michael, or shall I say, Pastor, will get it all together. He's the one in our relationship that usually gets the details together. He's always been good with that. I just need to find a place to sit and put up my weary feet. We've been in airports the better part of the day and it's cold as the dickens out here. Why they would have a conference in Chicago in the dead of the winter season is beyond me! I'm so tired and hungry I just want to go up to the room and rest my weary bones, but Episcopal Bishop Collins insist that we see him upon our arrival. Brenda, or whatever her name is, was asked to meet us in the lobby until his holiness makes a grand entrance to welcome us. With all the money Jehovah AME is bringing into the denomination, he would want to roll out the red carpet and have a grand feast prepared for us when we got here.

Lord knows I'd rather be home finishing up the plans for the women's retreat next week. The annual retreat is my responsibility and although I dread all the work that goes into it, once I get started I'm dedicated to the task. I need to meet with the team at least one more time to ensure all plans are still going smoothly. What I like most about the retreat is that it's an opportunity for the women of the church to come together and share the experience of "womanness". That's the theme of this year's retreat—Discover the Woman in You from the Eyes of God. We are strong and divinely made. All the cattiness and other nonsense we engage in is not what God wants from us. The more we focus on our purpose the happier and healthier we will be. This women's retreat promises to be even more life changing than last year. We had a mishap with the scheduling of one of the speakers last year, which is why I need to have a tighter rein this year. Good thing I was able to bring in my home girl, Linda Blanks, at the last minute to give the attendees a message on contentment in the single state. Many of the woman who attended were single or divorced and really needed to hear from a strong spiritual sister what it means to truly be content in the single state. She was awesome. Glory to God! We had a spirit-filled time in the Lord! I briefed Pastor every night of our 3-day stay and he was very pleased. He truly has a heart for the women of the church and if I was a sensitive woman, I wouldn't be very happy about that. He and Ezra share that sincere heart for people in general, which makes people flock to them like magnets. Pastor also cares very much for the male seed and making sure they are strengthened in the Lord. After all, they are the core of the family foundation. If the foundation isn't stable, the whole family will suffer. But every now and then, some woman will take his kindness for something other than its intention and that's when I have to step in and straighten them out!

Finally! There's the grand pooh-bah himself. Let me stand up so we can get this over with. Look at him grinning from ear to ear. Reminds me of a possum. He's slick like one, too. They smile in Pastor's face and behind closed doors try to figure out how they can control him and his ministry. Well, the folks at Jehovah AME absolutely love their pastor and—

"Sister Foster! How are you?"

"Doing well, Bishop Collins. Good to see you."

"We're going to have a fine time in the Lord, Amen? Praise God! Everything is in place. I anticipate this conference will be the best one ever, yes saa."

Bishop Collins is full of it!

"Bishop Collins, we certainly are looking forward to a very productive conference in light of our agenda."

Listen to my husband! Just as cool as he want to be! Before he got involved, the conference agenda was a complete mess. That's why they asked him to step in. He pulled the whole conference together. Organized it practically from scratch . . . got the right speakers lined up, and now it's going to be a success largely due to his hard work and the fact that he is truly anointed. He sincerely knows and loves the Lord and that's what it takes to be fruitful. You have to know Him and have faith in Him.

"Why don't you two settle into your rooms? Pastor Foster if you wouldn't mind meeting me here in an hour, I want to talk to you about the agenda changes that were just made."

What!

"Is there something wrong? Did someone cancel on us?"

"No, no . . . nothing like that. WE just thought there needed to be some tweaking here and there to maximize the purpose of why we are here. Go ahead and get settled. I'll see you in an hour."

Ain't that nothing! First of all, the agenda was approved four months ago and there was a final meeting three weeks ago to ensure everything was in place. Second, why in the world would someone want to tamper with an agenda of this magnitude on the eve of the event! Thirdly, who is WE? I bet it's the same four southern pastors that are dead set in wreaking havoc on our ministry. Lord, if jealousy had a face it would be theirs, including that Bishop Collins! Furthermore, why couldn't they wait to consult with Pastor before making changes? Pastor's going to get an earful from me as soon as the elevator doors close.

Is that my cell phone?

"Hello?"

"Hi, Momma."

"Hey, Mickey. How you doing, son?"

"Great. You guys make it to Chicago, OK? I hear the weather's really bad there."

"Yea. Someone told the weather authority that a bunch of preachers were making their way over here and they decided to bring out an extra dose of bad weather. Hold on a second. Your Dad is chomping at the bit to talk to you."

That Mickey is a good son and that grandson of mine is a chip off the ole block. I love that boy to death. Good thing he inherited a lot from this side of the family. Michal is just as smart as a whip, and handsome too. Got those killer hazel-green eyes like his Daddy. They both got 'em from me. Mickey promised to let Michal spend a few weeks over the summer with us, but the jury's still out on that. Claudette said something about some expensive science camp she wants to send Michal to, and said she would get back to us. I won't bet money on it. She is so jealous of the special bond Michal and I share that it drives her crazy! I'm at a loss for words when it comes to that woman. She's in her mid 40s and so mixed up and confused it doesn't make sense. Got a hint of that Island blood in her, which should be a good thing, but she's just as unstable as a coon dog on a jackrabbit! I also can't stand the fact that she's much older than Mickey. Why couldn't she find someone her own age? I'll give her one thing. She knows a good catch when she sees it. Just scooped Mickey right on up. I don't think the boy saw it coming, but I did. I could see it the minute he introduced her to me. I would have told him, too, but he didn't ask me.

Finally, the room!!!! Pastor is still on the line with our eldest. Must be pretty important. I'm going to take a nice long bath, order a canteen of coffee and wait to hear what Pastor has to say about this last minute agenda change crap. No telling what those vipers have cooked up, but I'll be here ready and waiting to help "MY Pastor" deal with it. Yes indeed. Me and Pastor have seen many a day together and it wasn't all rosy either. Real tried and true, heartbreaking stuff. Don't want to even think of it now, but one thing I know for sure . . . you can get through anything if you believe in it. I believe in my husband and I believe in us. No matter how many times I sliced it, life is so much better to go through with him in it. Sure it was hard to follow his calling, especially since I hadn't heard from God to start a church. I had to have trust and faith in my husband that he had truly heard from God in order to follow that plan. It was hard to put the second and third mortgage on the house to build the first church home and many times I looked at Michael as if he had three heads. In the end, I had faith in his faith. Now 35 years later our church has the biggest congregation on the East coast. Praise be to God! Through it all, we've been a solid team. Our strengths and weaknesses complement each other and when the smoke clears, we know we have each other's back. As the young people say, 'that's how we roll'!

Acknowledgements

Inspiration and encouragement are two very important elements to any endeavor. I would be remiss if I didn't give thanks to those who directly and indirectly provided the inspiration and encouragement necessary to see this project through.

I thank God for my family. To my parents, William and Emerante Hall, who taught me so much about love, life and relationships. I have learned so much through the course of writing this book as a result of our discussions. Thank you for your honesty and for sharing your experiences.

They say your brothers and sisters can be your worst critics and your best friends. Well . . . that's true! To my brothers and sisters, Richard, Torleta, Pamela, Billy, Ronnie, Jeffrey, Christopher, and Christina, thank you for sharing this invaluable journey with me. Love you all!

I want to thank my brothers and sisters-in-laws for your part in strengthening our family tree (trust me, I have interviewed folks who didn't want to have anything to do with their in-laws). You played an invaluable part in raising my beautiful nieces and nephews, who have truly captured my heart. So to Felicia, Rob, Samantha, Pierre, Kimberly, Kenny, Ariel, Malaika, Kaila, Tylar, Devon, Jeff, Jade, Madison, Kaleb, Brooke, Me-me, and little Gabby, Auntie V (Dee-Dee) loves you very much! Keep striving.

A special thank you to my Pastor and First Lady, Bob and Yolanda Wingfield of Woodstream Church in Mitchellville, MD. Thank you for presenting the uncompromising Word of God every Sunday and for your inspiring example of faithfulness. Thanks also to my church family at Woodstream. You welcomed us into the church family with open arms and I thank God for your love and support.

To my "adoptive" sisters, Sherelle Williams, Kinyette Newman, and Monique Lindsay, your sisterly bond and counsel are immeasurable. To my "soul" sister J. Kathy (Twin) Everett—our years of sisterhood and friendship is like fine wine.

Thanks to everyone who shared thoughts, experiences, and ideas that contributed to the making of this book. I won't call your names out here because it is far too many of you to name and I fear I might miss someone. Continue on the voyage of love seeking your heart's desires through the Word of God.

Much love to the 2010 graduating class of American University's Graduate Film and Video program. We survived! Now let's make some movies!

To Charles and Carmen Mosby, I can't tell you how thankful I am for your support and love for Christian and me. Your love relationship of 47 years has been an invaluable example for both of us and we are blessed to have you in our lives.

To my Link Inc., sisters of the Annapolis Chapter, thank you for your love and support. Your extension of friendship and sisterhood touches my heart and I am grateful to be a part of "the circle".

Annabelle Lockhart, Dr. Patsy B. Blackshear, Charles Pugh, Ceil Holmes, Sam Mok, and Anne Baird-Bridges your friendship and mentorship through the years have been priceless. I am honored to call you friends, and brothers and sisters in Christ.

Victoria Christopher Murray you are a rock star! Thank you for your support and sage advice in helping me to maneuver through this writing thang! I'm certain I speak for many when I say you are an inspiration to us all. I continue to grow as a writer because of you.

Kwame Alexander, Tina McElroy Ansa, Parry "Ebony Satin" Brown, Connie Briscoe, Tinesha Davis, Virginia DeBarry, Eric Jerome Dickey, Jamellah Ellis, Lolita Files, Juan Gaddis, Donna Grant, Donna Hill, Kevin Wayne Johnson, R.M. Johnson, Booker T. Mattison, and Monda Webb many thank you's for your inspiration and support. You are all soldiers in the literary world protecting literacy and churning out quality and thought-provoking work. Let's continue to press!

To the folks at Trafford Publishing, and the management team at Phoenix Rizen—you are top notch!

To Rodney, whose love sustains and inspires me. Experiencing the season of love with you has been enriching and has elevated my understanding of what true love really is. I am indelibly changed by our connection. My love . . . my heart.

To my son, Christian, who inspires me beyond words and never ceases to amaze me. Your love and profound wisdom has lifted me to heights I pray every Mom can experience through her children. Thank you for your unending love and support. I thank the Lord for you always. Love You!

To anyone I have left out, please charge my negligence to the late hour in which I penned this section and not my heart. My appreciation for you is immeasurable. You can definitely take that to the bank and cash it!

Lastly and most importantly, to my heavenly Father above, who promised to never leave or forsake me. To you I am eternally grateful and humbled. You have provided for me, and continue to make clear the path of "purpose". As I walk this road, mine is a confident and comfortable stride because your love has not only made me *free*, it has made me *complete*.

V. Helena

Excerpt

When I'm Ready

Anticipated release: Fall 2012

Carmen Johnson is a relationship columnist with her own syndicated radio show headquartered in Washington, DC. Always one to give great relationship advice, she often falls short on reaping the benefits of her own advice . . . until Pastor Cory Madison comes into her life. Cory, a charismatic preacher with a growing ministry is just what the doctor ordered . . . handsome, charming, and faithful—a combination that has eluded Carmen's pick of men in the past. Just as it appeared wedding bells would be ringing for the power couple, in walks Miles Davidson. Miles is the successful attorney that stole Carmen's heart five years prior only to fade to black after choosing his blossoming career over a future with her. Now faced with losing the love she'd always hoped for or taking another chance on love, Carmen has to make a life changing and everlasting decision . . . but is she ready? Using the setting of the nation's capitol as a backdrop, this formidable tale spins a web of betrayal and redemption about real life situations and outcomes.

Where's My Valentine?

Carmen put on headphones and waited for her producer, Patrick, to cue her back on the air. She quickly took another swig of the hot lemon tea she was nursing and nodded to acknowledge the countdown. 3.2.1

"Hello, DC! This is your girl, Carmen Johnson, coming back at ya with the 411 on relationships. Can I get an Amen? The lines are blowing up and I think I only have time for one or two more calls. Again, the question of the day is, why am I spending Valentine's Day alone?

I have Tammy from Hyattsville on the line. Tammy, what's your story?"

"Hi, Carmen. Are ya there?" Tammy said with a strong Washingtonian accent. Her voice was echoing in the background.

"I hear ya, Tammy, but I need you to turn your radio down, ok? Are you alone this Valentine's Day weekend?"

"Yes. I broke up with my boyfriend a few weeks ago and I thought we'd be back together by now, but I guess he's gone for good this time," Tammy said with a hint of melancholy.

"What happened, Tammy?" Carmen said before taking another sip from her mug.

"Well. I was . . . I guess you could say I was being petty. Me and my boyfriend have been together for five years and we've been living together for almost two.

"Ok. Stop right there," Carmen interrupted. "You're living with this man unmarried".

"Well . . . Yes," Tammy said hesitantly.

"Um-hmm. Continue," Carmen said in her "sister-girl" tone. Tammy let out a short giggle.

"Well, in the first year of living together, I didn't bring up marriage because . . . honestly, I was ok with just living together. I saw it as a trial basis to see if we could actually live together and make it work. So he didn't bring it up, and to be fair, I didn't either."

"Uh-huh. So you're taking some ownership of the situation you eventually found yourself in. That's good," Carmen interjected.

"Yes. So a few weeks ago, my cousin got married and we went out of town to his wedding. Some of my peeps were asking me when me and Charles, that's my ex's name, were planning to tie the knot because . . . you know . . . that was the expectation since we've been together so long."

"Uh-huh," Carmen said as she wrote notes on her pad.

"So, because my family at the wedding were asking about when we were going to take the plunge, I brought it up on the drive back home."

"Hmmm. And what was his reaction?" Carmen said adjusting her glasses on her nose.

"He wanted to know why was it so important what my family had to say about our relationship," Tammy said.

"Out of curiosity, how long was the drive home?"

"We were coming back in from Philly, so I guess about 2 ½ hours, maybe a little longer."

"Ok. So how did the conversation end and how did you get where you are today?"

"Well. The conversation didn't go well at all. We argued almost all the way home, and I really feel as though he wasn't listening or understanding my point. He just kept focusing on my family and saying how nosey they are, which made me very angry. I reminded him that we were talking about getting married, once upon a time, and that now that we've been together for so long, we should really consider where we are going with this relationship."

"Wow. This is a common mistake we make as women. We set up house and live the life of a married person without the ring, then expect the ring to quickly follow. It's rare when that works out for us. In most cases it doesn't, and there are stats to prove it, sweetie," Carmen offered.

"I know, but I really thought we were on the same page," Tammy said quietly.

"It's good that you addressed the subject directly. So tell me how this all lead to you being alone on Valentine's Day?"

"I didn't bring it up again until about two weeks ago. We had just gotten back from having dinner with friends in Georgetown and he was watching TV when I asked him if we could talk. I brought up marriage and he was completely on the defensive. He straight out told me he wasn't ready and he couldn't explain why or what that meant. I told him I didn't want to continue living together without a plan and he told me, 'I gotta do what I gotta do.' So last week, I moved out."

"I'm sorry to hear that, Tammy. Did he ever tell you why he wasn't ready or why he thought he may have been ready before when you two were actively talking about it?"

"No. He just said he wasn't ready and he pretty much shut down after that," said Tammy a little choked up.

"What do you want right now, Tammy?"

"I want my man back!"

"Are you willing to wait until he's ready."

"I don't know what that even means . . . when I'm ready," Tammy said in a huff.

Carmen sat back in her chair for a moment as she heard Tammy continue to lament about her situation. Hearing Tammy pour out her heart took Carmen back to the dilemma she was in two years ago with Miles Davidson, a man she once considered her soul-mate and the love of her life. Sadly, their relationship ended under similar circumstances, and now she has a second chance at love with Cory Madison, her pastor and boyfriend of nine months. She smiled knowing he would be waiting for her after she signed off the air.

"Well, in short order, although you had been talking about marriage before you moved in together, it doesn't sound as though living together was part of the overall marriage plan," Carmen said interrupting Tammy's tirade. "If you moved in to save for a scheduled wedding, that *might* qualify as being part of a marriage plan. Instead, it sounds as though you were both test driving this thing and perhaps one or both of you decided that you were comfortable with the current status of the relationship."

"Well, all I know is I love him and I want to get married," Tammy said with determination.

"I hear ya, girly. Here's my advice to you. When *you're* ready, invite him over for dinner . . . I know you know his favorites by now, right?"

"Yea, I know what he likes and how he likes it," Tammy said giggling.

"Great! Have him come over and after dinner, have a pressure free conversation with him, not about marriage but about what's important to you right now in the relationship. It sounds as though you want him back and you want to work through this impasse. Am I right?" Carmen said cuing Patrick for the time left in the segment.

"You're dead on," Tammy said with renewed confidence.

"Ok. So without judgment and with an ear to listen, listen to what he has to say about all of this. It sounds as though the conversations the two of you have been having have ended with his reaction as opposed to hearing what he has to say about the situation. Many times, men are not as forthcoming in verbalizing their feelings in love relationships, particularly if they feel threatened or pressured. I think the two of you may be surprised with the outcome of that conversation. You may walk away with a better understanding of his feelings and perhaps it will bring you closer together. There is also the chance that it will not end the way you would like for it to end. You have to be prepared for that possibility, too. If it doesn't work out, throw this experience in your bag of experiences and grow from it. Ok, Tammy?"

"Ok. That sounds cool."

"And one other thing," Carmen said coming in closer to the mic.

"What's that?"

"If you get back together, don't move back in. Shacking up can be a prescription for disaster in any relationship. Statistics confirm it and honestly he seemed to be on course to marriage until you moved in together."

"I see what you're saying," Tammy said.

"And were you practicing celibacy?"

"Um no," Tammy said shyly.

"It may seem difficulty, but it's possible as long as you're convicted about living for Christ," Carmen adjusting her glass.

"Yes, Ma'am," Tammy giggled.

"Great! Keep me posted on how things work out for you. Give me a call, email or post it on my blog." Carmen saw the wrap up signal from Patrick. "Ok. Tammy's my last caller, folks. I'll be back with my final thoughts."

Carmen took off the headphones as someone handed her a note—
Running late with a ministry meeting. Will call when I get out. Cory

Carmen smiled as she bawled up the note and shot it into the trash can.

"Great topic today. Phones stayed lit for the duration of the show," Patrick said into the microphone of the soundroom across from Carmen.

"Love is always a great topic for discussion", Carmen said while writing notes on her tablet. "Valentine's Day only makes it even more eventful. Big plans tonight?

"Sherrie and I are going to do what we usually do, sit in front of the TV with popcorn watching a chick flick," Patrick said with a grin.

"Now isn't that adorable!" Carmen said taking a last swig of her now lukewarm tea. "Enjoy!"

"Yea, right . . . Ok and you're on in 5 . . . 4 . . . 3 . . . 2 . . . 1."

"Well thank you for your calls tonight, and thanks for inviting me into your heart on this cold, but beautiful Valentine's Day night. We heard from a lot of you—married and single—who are spending your lover's holiday alone. Psalm 37:4 says, *delight yourself in the Lord and He will give you the desires of your heart.* Stay encouraged, and stay open to the possibilities of love. Wherever it finds you, be ready to receive it, and when you have it, make the best of it because it doesn't promise to be with you always. It does promise to be as fulfilling as you'll make it, so do it up! I'll be back next weekend to take your love calls. Have a great V-Day and be safe out there."

After saying goodnight to everyone, Carmen gathered her things and was about to put on her coat when her friend, Sheila Banks, walked into the studio.

"Hey, girly! Great show. What's up for tonight?"

"Thanks. Well, I was planning to catch up with Cory after the show, but he's delayed. What's cooking with you?"

"Girl, I wish something was cooking with me," Sheila said helping Carmen with her coat. "I should have called into your show tonight."

"Why? What's up with you and Gary?"

"We're good . . . I guess. He's hanging out with his boys tonight. I'll see him tomorrow."

"Really . . . ok," Carmen said in an attempt to remain neutral as they walked down the hall to the parking lot.

"You don't think that's weird?" Sheila said baiting her.

"It doesn't matter what I think, now does it," Carmen said playfully raising an eyebrow.

"Well, you know what I mean. He's not into the 'lovey-dovey Valentine's Day bull-crap', as he calls it. It's just another Friday and he's hanging with the boys."

"Ok . . . that's cool . . . as long as you're cool with it."

"Well, I'm not totally, but you know. What can I say?"

"Whatever you feel you should say . . . but for now, just say yes to a chili smoke from Ben's Chili Bowl. I'm starving!" Carmen said getting into her car. Sheila giggled and jumped into the passenger seat.

Back at her apartment, Carmen gazed out at the spectacular, panoramic water-view of the Potomac River from her National Harbor condo. The private boats had started their romantic sojourn towards Virginia and other points in Washington, DC and Maryland. She made a mental note to treat her BFF, Katrina Holmes, to a water taxi ride over to Old Town Alexandria when she arrived from New York in a few weeks. Katrina insisted on flying down to help unpack the mess of boxes that littered the sparsely furnished 12th floor abode. Carmen sighed heavily at the thought of unpacking what was thrown together in haste. Although the decision to move back home to Washington, DC was thoughtfully calculated, her packing was not.

Carmen was elated when she received the call from Howard University to host their new Saturday night radio talk show, Good Love. Although the original idea behind the show was to discuss relationships in general, Carmen wowed the producers when she brought in the spin on Christian dating.

"Kind of a Saturday night bible study on relationships," she said proudly.

Carmen didn't think they were interested until she received the call three weeks later from the producer and was asked if she could be back in DC within a month. Carmen loved living in New York and working for the NY Times as a relationship columnist, but saw the radio show as a career opportunity that could not be missed.

Aside from being overjoyed with the idea of being back in her hometown with family and friends, she was especially happy about cultivating her relationship with her new beau, Cory Madison. She had known Cory since he was a minister at her family's church, Agape AME. When his father fell ill and stepped down as pastor, Cory took up the mantel and has been serving as pastor for the past three years. Whenever she was home, Carmen would attend Sunday service with her Mom, and enjoyed Cory's sermons. About a year ago, Cory started to inquiry about Carmen to her mother.

"He asked about me?" Carmen said incredulously.

"Sure! I was waiting for your Dad to bring the car around and we were talking and he asked about you," Carmen's Mom said with enthusiasm.

"Well, that's not unusual, Mom. He's asking because he's our pastor, I'm sure."

"He reads your column, too."

"Really!"

"That's what he said. I think he's impressed by the scriptural foundation of your articles. I told him that came from me," Carmen's Mom said proudly.

"Right," Carmen said laughing into the phone. "Well, maybe I can talk to him about it while I'm home for the holidays in a few weeks."

"I think he'd like that," Carmen's Mom said grinning ear-to-ear.

Her conversation with Cory in the church parking lot turned into dinner a week later. He was very impressed with her views on relationships and her passion in ensuring God's message was released to anyone who would hear it. She was doubly impressed with his conviction and dedication to service and living in purpose. After a few months, Carmen found herself in a full blown relationship with her pastor, and was loving every minute of it. Now that she was living in DC, she anticipated their relationship growing stronger. She hadn't really dated since the break up with Miles, and the physical distance between she and Cory helped her to pace and better appreciate her relationship with him. Cory was different from any other man she dated, and she was certain their relationship was meant to be.

As she lifted the screaming teakettle from the heating element, Carmen checked her cell phone to see if Cory had sent a text message on his status. She had hoped they would have an early start on their weekend, but knew Cory had to be attentive to church business when duty called. She thought about sprucing up her apartment a little before he came over, but decided on second thought to wait for Katrina's help.

Carmen was just about to go back to her bedroom when she heard the doorbell.

"Finally," she yelled and headed for the door. Without looking through the peephole, she flung open the door ready to throw herself into Cory's arms, but lost her balance suddenly.

"Hey, Lady," Miles said holding a bottle of White Merlot in one hand and a box of Valentine candy in the other.

* * *

When I'm. Ready
will be in stores Fall 2012.

About The Author

An accomplished author, film producer, director, screenwriter, playwright, and business-woman, V. Helena has been writing creatively for over 20 years. A graduate of the University of Maryland, Marymount University, and American University, this Haitian-American has secured degrees in the areas of radio, television, film, business administration, and law. After accepting her calling to write for the Lord in May 2001, she immediately turned her efforts towards faith-based literary writing and film production. She also established Phoenix Rizen, LLC, a film and video production company headquartered in Maryland. Her years of writing experience has spawned two books, as well as her first novel effort entitled, **When I'm Ready**, due out in stores in Fall 2012. V. Helena lives in Maryland with her family.

To learn more about the author, you may visit her on the web at www.vhelena.com.

Reading References

As part of my research in writing this book, I came across many publications that served as useful guides. Here are a few that would be worthwhile to add to your reading collection.

1. **The Five Love Languages**, by Gary Chapman
2. **Can Two Walk Together**, by Sabrina D. Black
3. **The Purpose Driven Life**, by Rick Warren
4. **If Men are Like Buses**, by Michelle McKinney Hammond
5. **The Best Kind of Loving**, by Dr. Gwendolyn Goldsby Grant
6. **Understanding the Purpose and Power of Woman**, by Dr. Myles Monroe
7. **Understanding the Purpose and Power of Man**, by Dr. Myles Monroe
8. **Sacred Pampering Principles**, by Debra Jackson Gandy
9. **Making Sense of the Men in Your Life**, by Dr. Kevin Leman

Autographed Copies and Speaking Engagements

To receive an autographed copy of **His Love Is Freedom** or **His Love Is Complete,** please email V. Helena at <u>author@vhelena.com</u>.

All requests for speaking engagements should be directed to the Management Division of Phoenix Rizen, LLC at <u>info@phoenixrizen.com</u>.

<u>www.vhelena.com</u>